BAAS Pamphlets in American Studies 25

Language Poetry and the American Avant-garde

Geoff Ward

British Association for American Studies

First Published 1993

© British Association for American Studies, 1993

ISBN 0 946488 15 0

Composed and originated by Ryburn Publishing Services
Printed by Ryburn Book Production, Keele University, Keele, Staffordshire

Contents

1. Introduction

This study has a double focus. The rise to critical prominence in the United States of the so-called 'Language' poets is both remarkable in itself, and a development that sets the achievements and dominant styles of postwar American Poetry in a new, and a questionable light. What follows is first of all a critical introduction to Language poetry; to its origins, personnel, stated aims, and distinguishing features of method and content.

Although the group includes one or two elders such as Clark Coolidge and Michael Palmer who, as it were, wrote poetry before there was Language, this development has brought to public attention a range of authors equal if only in their unfamiliarity to non-American readers: to mention Ron Silliman, Steve Benson, Lyn Hejinian, Susan Howe, Barrett Watten, Leslie Scalapino, Stephen Rodefer, Craig Watson, Steve McCaffery, Bob Perelman, Robert Grenier, Hannah Weiner and Diane Ward would by no means exhaust the list of salient contributors. Jerome McGann, a sympathetic onlooker, takes the view that in Language writing 'poetry appears at a crisis of its traditional modes of expression.'[1] Rod Mengham detects a utopian impulse in the will-to-crisis, seeing in the Language group's aggressive deconstruction of literary subjectivity an ambitious and (if it works) fundamental reorientation of the relations between poem, writer, and reader, 'bringing to an end the long history of poetry which privileges the writer's mind'. The new poem will include *ab initio* 'a preconception of how, when and where it will be read.'[2] (Apparent echoes of Reception Theory and poststructuralist accounts of the writing process are not coincidental, and will bear investigation at a later stage.)

It would be easy to show the divergence of Language poetry from the more conservative traditions of American verse; a Language poem looks and sounds nothing like a poem by Robert Lowell or James Dickey or Louise Glück. More vexed, and likely to prove of greater historical consequence, is the relationship between Language writing and the various postwar American avant-gardes; the Beats, the Black Mountain or New York schools. The generation of Robert Creeley or Ed Dorn, writers born for the most part in the 1920s, had managed by and large to hang on to its radical and progressive credentials until the 1980s – until, that is, the advent of Language poetry. Before turning to the poetry of today, it may be useful to sketch once more the literary terrain of the postwar period in which that earlier radicalism took root.

II

The poetic consensus in America, one that held steady for around forty years, involved the antagonistic but balanced co-existence of an establishment literature (epitomised first by Auden, finally by Lowell) and a loosely left-Bohemian opposition, represented by Donald Allen's famous anthology *The New American Poetry*.[3] The New American Poets had their own hierarchies and preacher or teacherly figures (Robert Duncan, Charles Olson), but retained a fraternal proximity to the counter-culture and spirit of rebelliousness that reached its maximum level of social diffusion in the late 1960s. Like the aroused lovers and sprightly musicians depicted on Keats's Grecian Urn, these poets were frozen in time; doomed never to win, to topple the poetic establishment, but allowed to keep their Dionysiac wildness, and an air of dangerous experimentalism. Although the huge *Collected Poems of Allen Ginsberg* comes complete with a name and subject index, while the photograph on the dustjacket bestows on its subject all the glamour of a retired banker, Ginsberg would until very recently have been the poet most identified with 'youth' by America's reading public. The moment of Language poetry is therefore a critical moment for the whole post-1945 period in American poetry. The poetic Urn – be it Well-Wrought and classical or the Dionysiac kind – would at long last appear to have been broken. In the chapters that follow, I will ask whether the *soi-disant* vanguardism of the City Lights generation is given a decisive knock by Language; are Ginsberg and John Ashbery (whose influence and prominence since the mid-1970s loom larger than Lowell's ever did) merely the new Establishment? Are the Language writers, Blasting and Making It New in the poetry stakes, just the latest wave of New American Poets who will one day be comfortably assimilated into the old?

III

The generation that came to prominence in the late 50s and early 60s was divided internally according to geographical region. The Beats were associated chiefly with the West Coast, finding a supportive context in San Francisco's traditional tolerance towards homosexuality, as well as the literature of psychic exploration and political dissent initiated by the 'San Francisco Renaissance' of Kenneth Rexroth and his contemporaries.[4] By contrast the New York School (Frank O'Hara, John Ashbery, James Schuyler et al) pursued careers in the art world that brought them into contact with Abstract Expressionist painting, as well as the influence of immigrant Surrealists, and the side of New York culture which has always endeavoured to face Europe rather than the Americas.[5] Meanwhile in the backwoods of Carolina, its last rector, Charles Olson, was fighting to keep Black Mountain College open for a Faculty of independent minds that had included Robert Duncan and John Cage; Robert Creeley, an external examiner who stayed: and a student body barely younger than its teachers, that included Edward Dorn, Fielding Dawson, and John Wieners.

It is important to note that each of these separate regions maintained its own particular access to publication and dissemination of work. The differences in typography, page-size and other design features, that distinguish the books published by Lawrence Ferlinghetti at the City Lights Bookstore in San Francisco from, say, the early pamphlets by Ashbery or O'Hara appearing under the imprint of the Tibor de Nagy Gallery in New York, could not be greater. Each carries its own cultural associations which bear on wider social issues, as well as the politics of poetry.

Michael Davidson speaks for a whole generation of poetry readers when he recalls 'an older "bohemian" student' lending him a City Lights Pocket Poets volume on a school bus in 1959.

> Not only had I never read poems like that (we were still trying to figure out why the horse *did* stop in the woods on a snowy evening), I had never seen books made like that. Its small format and stapled binding bespoke a portability intended for immediate access, a book one was meant to read on the bus or standing in line. And there was something about the way my friend handed the book to me that signaled secrecy and solidarity at the same time.[6]

A few years earlier, John Bernard Myers' gallery in New York had published *Turandot*, a pamphlet of poems by John Ashbery now so rare and sought-after that even its author does not possess a copy. At the time, however, Myers' enthusiasm for the new poetry was not shared by visitors to the gallery. While abstract canvasses costing thousands of dollars were a chic acquisition (and a reminder of the new American triumphalism), the pamphlet costing two dollars didn't sell. Where the West Coast poetry book was a sign of the burgeoning counter-culture, building on a regional tradition of political dissidence, the East Coast book was at best a de luxe adornment.

Of course, to paraphrase a line from John Ashbery, these distinctions can be brought to life in order to be dismantled. A simple geographical model of the contesting poetries and poetics brought together in the Allen anthology will not quite do. The contradictions are multiple: *Lunch Poems*, the most popular collection by New York poet Frank O'Hara, was published by City Lights in San Francisco. Ginsberg, the poetic voice of the West Coast, has lived for many years in New York, and his work contains far more references to that city than does, for example, John Ashbery's. An historical account of Robert Duncan's development would need to place him in the mutually inimical contexts of Black Mountain College, with its house-style of austere self-sufficiency and heterosexist swagger, and the more bardically exotic Berkeley Renaissance of Brother Antoninus and the gay, Orphic poet Jack Spicer. In fact, the lines along which the geographical distinctions do hold, and had purpose, are ultimately not to do with physical locale, but with procedural antipathies. The Beats, the New Yorkers and the Black Mountaineers liked to be seen to be at odds with each other on methodological and political grounds. The claim of each côterie to prime visibility was strengthened by the combative assertion of its differences from rival groups.

Frank O'Hara, for example, condemned the Black Mountain addiction to 'the serious utterance, which isn't particularly desirable most of the time', seeing in Charles Olson's *Maximus Poems* a congested neo-Poundian gravitas that could only sit in the reader's way.[7] In his mock-manifesto 'Personism', included by Donald Allen in the anthology, O'Hara dismissed the contemporary agonising over linebreaks and questions of form that had spread in the wake of Olson's 'Projective Verse' manifesto: 'You just go on your nerve. If someone's chasing you down the street with a knife you just run, you don't turn around and shout, "Give it up! I was a track star for Mineola Prep."'[8] Yet O'Hara's poems didn't 'just run', or if they did it was along and then beyond pathways explored by the French Surrealists. André Breton and his followers were important precursors of the New York group through the mediating influence of the art world, in which O'Hara and Ashbery had begun successful middle-class careers, the former as assistant and then associate curator at the Museum of Modern Art. John Bernard Myers of the Tibor Gallery had been the managing editor of *View*, Breton's journal-in-exile. As a result of such professional connections, Allen Ginsberg and others were able to accuse the New York côterie of East Coast snobbery with a European bias. Ginsberg's elegy for Frank O'Hara (killed in an accident in 1966) mixes tenderness and regret with a sharp attack on O'Hara's milieu, in particular its supporting cast of Ivy League brahmins on the make:

> I tried   your boys and found them ready
> > sweet and amiable
> > > collected gentlemen
> > > > with large sofa apartments
> > > lonesome to please   for pure language:
> > and you mixed with money
> > > > because you knew enough language to be rich[9]

Here we see the reopening of old antagonisms. Ginsberg's disinclination to adopt a 'pure language' returns us to the agenda of Walt Whitman (his chief rhetorical influence) and William Carlos Williams (his mentor), in calling for a severance of pioneering American poetics from Europe and the Old World. With all three poets, this call was the literary expression of a dissident politics. Yet, if O'Hara 'mixed with money', Allen Ginsberg's own radicalism was nothing if not mixed, as his programme for sexual and psychic liberation came to dissolve in the deluded and diluted Romanticism of a 60s hippy culture it had helped to create. These ironies and arguments have been well charted, and it is not the aim of this study to repeat them. It will be more helpful to examine the ways in which the emergence and intervention of Language poetry have shunted all those debates and procedural antagonisms into a new light and, perhaps, a new vulnerability, one that emphasizes the *affinities* between the New American Poets at the expense of the internal differences on which they themselves tended to dwell.

IV

The early poems of Steve Benson show the crude, innovative power of Language poetry in the 1970s. Their rhetorical strategies are drastic, and initiate a critique of Benson's poetic precursors:

I want to go out for love tonight
If you want to get existential a moment
Fabricate a lie darling
This crisp determinate, silvery bill
Glance into the fat of my hand
('"I want to go out for love tonight …"')

the hair along her navel to vagina line feels like tingling
9 persons found dead on freeway early this morning
metal plates in the street I never consider their function
just flip pages in the dictionary forget the word adjudicate
alongside the room grazes a treetop birds swing out from
nylon hose flung out the window in mild abandon
let me read you this aloud

('As Is')[10]

The poetry's jaded undercutting of a romanticization of self and its affections is undercut in its turn: does 'This', in the first excerpt, refer to the 'lie'? What then, if anything, can truly be said to be 'determinate' here? Linguistic reference is angled sufficiently sharply to be a personal issue, but never within a specific social context – or even a specifically gendered context, as the 'her' that ends a later line shifts at once into 'Him the man I'm sitting next to'. The poem's constant recourse to a feint of reference, followed by a glancing blow, leaves us with a free-floating anxiety of agency, the unplaceability of what might signify 'love' and what 'a lie' exemplifying its inextricably mixed pleasure and threat. In the second excerpt lines connoting pleasure and threat are more sharply distinguishable, from a readerly viewpoint, but the poet's laconic admission that this text may be on permanent vacation from literature's traditional functions and responsibilities ('forget the word adjudicate'), is counterbalanced by persistent reminders of the textuality of lyric poetry. 'let me read you this aloud', reminds us quite precisely that he can't. In sum, the devices of estrangement employed by the two texts are each other's mirroring opposite: the first implies an abdication of conventional literary control through its immersion in the weird twinning of sexual overtures and cynical withdrawal, where the second simply dumps the whole thing on the reader and says, *you* sort it out – if you want to.

The strategies may differ but certain literary antecedents are common to both. Benson's 'you' is a contemporary descendant of the 'you' of Apollinaire's *Zone*, and Eliot's 'Rhapsody on a Windy Night'. Punctuation may have gone, but the initial capital letter of each line in the first excerpt, the typical length and nearly toneless tone of both, do recall, however vestigially, the run of casually intimate invective in the French and Francophile lyric from Baudelaire through Rimbaud and Surrealism to Frank O'Hara. Apparently even that rhetorical vestige may have smelled too strongly of a 'pure language' to Benson. Also in the late 70s he produced a sequence called *Blindspots*; the title poem begins as follows:

[*"Heyyyy!" other
crowd noise –
individual voice
indistinguishable*]

there are problems
situations

there are ... illusions,
allusions ...
there are collusions ...

[*voices gradually
dying down in
crowd, individual
voice heard some-
times*]

there are situations
described in film several times

There was a race horse called Gunga Din.
He had a problem,
by his own definition.
So he changed his name
to Samson.
Then he felt that he had
another kind of situation.
So
he walked over to the foul line,
sort of eased over to the foul line,
knocked up against it,
handled it for a while with his fingers
till it began to flake
and fray against his fingers.

The italicised portions of the text are not stage directions, as in a drama, but transcriptions of an actual event. Anyone suspicious that the reader was to be set up as the dupe of a neo-Dadaist tease might well find their suspicions confirmed by the author's prefatory admission that *Blindspots* (which occupies seventeen pages of printed text) 'was an unrehearsed, improvised oral poem I spoke as I determined it, moving between the audience and a brick wall' in reaction to three stereo tapes by a collaborator, playing at the time.[11] During the last decade Benson has pushed this kind of risky strategy to legendary extremes: for a text entitled 'The Town of He', for example, committing to memory long passages from, among other sources, *Peter Pan*, Johnson's life of Swift, Thoreau's *Civil Disobedience* and Cabeza de Vaca's 1542 report to the King of Spain regarding his peregrinations from Florida to Mexico, in order to offer spontaneous oral recombinations of their contents for the delectation of the audience at New York's Ear Inn on an evening in May, 1985.

So Benson's handling of pre-existing materials in order to make them 'flake' and 'fray' even more, is not without its humorous side. Nor is it without seriousness, a seriousness related to that very pre-existence. By his own account Benson is 'passionately in love with conversation'. Lyn Hejinian has likewise noticed this shift of emphasis away from subjectivity, writing that Benson's work issues always 'from within a full milieu'. Benson's poetry offers a polemical reversal of the now traditional model of relations between poem, poet and reader. Conventionally, the act of writing establishes an individualised claim to certain experiences, the originality of the claim attested by a linguistically unusual array of expression, which may be retrospectively summarised as that poet's 'style'. The poem, by these dimming lights, is ultimately a privileging of mind over its objects. This position may be said to have had its heroic phase in the Romantic period, surviving along the various strata of Modernist poetics in a dwindling and anxious form. The manifest social inefficacy of poetry has tended, in a utilitarian age, to push its practitioners into the frail refuge of alienated subjectivity. Here the very removal of poetic style from other, more common forms of expression has become poetry's own subject and remaining consolation. By direct, indeed violent, contrast, Benson's work reverses this process, insisting (as does most if not all Language poetry) that the self is basically a construct of social networks, no free agent, but rather a living and breathing point of intersection for various social and historical pressures or codes. The element of madcap role-playing in Benson's work can be viewed as an exploded diagram of this social reality as exhibited by one speaker. Its background, its theoretical matrix is (was) that of scientific Marxism. Its artistic working-out in Benson's poetry is, interestingly, anything but assured; there is no purposeful subscription to a political manifesto, but rather a series of constantly changing postures of unease. The multiplicity of discourses that go to make up the single self are heard as simultaneous, and conflicting. Benson's 'conversation', his 'full milieu', is invariably troubled by 'the immense amount of motion that is a person's life'.[12]

Most Language poetry is less honestly awkward than Steve Benson's. The wry comedy of Ron Silliman's work, or the attractively patterned reminiscence of Lyn Hejinian's *My Life*, both of which will be discussed later, are easier to take. (Indeed, the Hejinian text appears to be everyone's favourite Language book, and the first to make it onto the syllabus.) Many of the suppositions of these works are shared by Benson's, but he does clarify certain facets of Language practice by so insistently going to extremes. Of particular significance is his use, stretched to the point of parody, of improvisatory techniques and a stress on orality, ('let me read you this aloud'), which were of course key points of procedure for the earlier generation of New American Poets.

V

Whatever their differences, the Black Mountain, Beat and New York Schools shared a commitment to poetry as individualistic expression. Partly a literary matter bound up with the persistence of Romanticism, this emphasis can also be read as a reaction to the sullen conformity of American life in the period of Cold War. A stress on self-expression and the right to a private language unites the poetry, painting and music of the postwar years. This was the period in which jazz found a new popularity and a new critical respect, with players like John Coltrane and Albert Ayler pushing the rhythmical innovations of

BeBop into fabulously extended improvisations, heard at the time as articulating all kinds of emotional, ethnic and mystically philosophical tensions. In fact, this was the age of improvisation; Ginsberg's and Jack Kerouac's 'spontaneous bop prosody', the drip paintings of Jackson Pollock and Willem de Kooning, John Cage's use of the aleatory to make each musical performance unique and, as 1950s monochrome fanned out into the peacock colours of the 60s, the collective improvisation of the 'happening' and the first Pop Festivals.

The 1970s, therefore, may be read with hindsight as a period of aftermath, in which individual careers were consolidated, but where artistic individualism as a trailblazing credo sank to the point of parody in the culture of narcissism exemplified and recorded by Andy Warhol. It is at this point that poets such as Steve Benson begin to publish and perform. One could read in his emphasis on spoken improvisation a manic extrapolation from, and subversion of, the improvisatory aesthetic laid down by the jazz saxophone, Charles Olson's emphasis on the breath in his Projective Verse essay, and the principles underlying Ginsberg's urge to 'set the noun and dash of consciousness together jumping'.[13] Michael Davidson has coined the useful term 'expressivism' to cover these artistic developments of the Cold War period. The following chapter will be an attempt to sketch a summary of Language theory and practice, and to test Davidson's dual hypothesis that 'language-writing offers the most thorough critique of expressivism in postwar writing, even while building upon the earlier generation's accomplishments'. Davidson may slightly exaggerate the case, in summarising postwar poetics as one in which 'muscular and physical response is valued over reflective or discursive moments', *tout court*.[14] *The Maximus Poems* are nothing if not discursive, and reflective. But Davidson has located what may prove to be the most significant turning point in American poetry for thirty years.

2. L=A=N=G=U=A=G=E: The Politics of Poetic Form

I

It seems appropriate at this point to put the New American Poetry on hold, in order to give a brief chronological account of the development of Language poetry, together with a précis of the theoretical debates and positions that the poets have wanted most frequently to put under close scrutiny. To move from theoretical essays to poems, rather than the other way about, is itself an acknowledgement of the heavy emphasis this movement has always laid on theory, discussion, teaching, and the opening of possible avenues from poetry to politics. The first published use of the term 'Language Poetry' may well have occurred in 1975, when Ron Silliman edited a selection of work by nine poets (including Bruce Andrews, Clark Coolidge, Robert Grenier and Silliman himself) for *Alcheringa* magazine. There Silliman writes of the poets associated with (now defunct) little press poetry magazines like *This*, *Big Deal* and *Tottel's* as 'Called variously 'language centred', 'minimal', 'nonreferential formalism', 'structuralist'. Not a *group* but a *tendency* in the work of many.'[15] By this time Stephen Rodefer had begun to publish poems which carried a wit and verbal agility sponsored by the New York School; and Steve McCaffery had produced an interesting early work, *'Ow's "Waif"*, the poems of which result from 'a calculated action *upon* a specific word-source or "supply-text"', a use of 'found' materials that clearly derives from the cut-ups of William Burroughs, and the work of John Cage.[16] McCaffery would go on to edit a special number of the journal *Open Letter* in 1977, though in the verdict of Lee Bartlett 'once again it seemed to argue not for a movement but rather for a disposition.'[17] That 'disposition' was more international at this early stage than it would be subsequently. Along with the Americans known to Silliman, one would want to cite Canadians such as McCaffery and Christopher Dewdney, and some maverick British poets such as Paul Buck, whose magazine *Curtains* was combatively interested in the political implications of an extremist use of language. The more inflammatory poems by John James were relevant at this point, as was the work of a number of poets resident at one time or another in Cambridge, and represented by its small presses and journals: Tom Raworth, for example, perhaps the most consistently interesting poet writing in Britain today: and at the younger end, poet-scholars like Rod Mengham, and the late Veronica Forrest-Thomson, whose work anticipates much of what has happened since. In fact her book *Poetic Artifice* was the direct catalyst of an important theoretical text by Charles Bernstein, *Artifice of Absorption*.

It was Bernstein, and his co-editor Bruce Andrews, who formalised the 'disposition' into something nearer a movement through the appearance of their bimonthly journal $L=A=\mathcal{N}=G=U=A=G=E$, the first issue of which appeared in February 1978. Devoted to poetics, the journal combined a fabulously elliptical house-style with the urgency of a bulletin; strict limits were set on the length of book-reviews, many of which run to a hundred words or less. The first third of this review of Kit Robinson by Gary Lenhart will convey the general flavour.

> You can fill in the spaces in these poems with facts, as Kit Robinson does in "7 Days in Another Town." You only lose the special music like the wind everywhere in these pages. Discrete vowels poke no

Hollowness of Language's socialist claims

holes. No tantrums hack. Restrained verse turns credible, mostly jump jump.[18]

It certainly made a change from the *TLS*. Short pieces on Marx, schizophrenic discourse, and the performance of poetry appeared alongside a putative revision of the canon, entailing respectful notices of new work by John Ashbery, and reassessments of Louis Zufosky and the late Laura (Riding) Jackson. Gertrude Stein's *Tender Buttons* (1914) found a new prominence.

Summarizing the magazine's different projects, its editors were to lay stress on an orientation for L=A=N=G=U=A=G=E beyond Language poetry alone; Bernstein and Andrews drew attention to

> our analysis of the capitalist social order as a whole and of the place that alternative forms of writing and reading might occupy in its transformation. It is our sense that the project of poetry does not involve turning language into a commodity for consumption; instead, it involves repossessing the sign through close attention to, and active participation in, its production.[19]

There are two things to note here, before moving forward into an engagement with the argument as such. From a European perspective at any rate, this would appear to be the first group-resurgence of a specifically socialist programme in American letters since the 30s. But if L=A=N=G=U=A=G=E is taken at its word, as returning to an agenda of revolution for the dispossessed, rather than libertarianism for the disaffected, as in 60s campus unrest, this is still a discourse shaped by the university. The Marxist lexicon of commodity fetishism and the social order is filtered by a vocabulary that derives from the various developments in literary criticism since 1968. As a matter of historical fact, L=A=N=G=U=A=G=E was the first published, collective evidence of the impact of what university literature departments now summarise as 'theory' on the practise of poetry in America.

The achievements, characteristic range of style, and the crucial dilemmas of Language writing were there from its inception in the late 70s, in this journal. Here were to be found: a project for massive social change; a collective project to write and to analyze poetry in relation to the impact of European theory; and the attempt to yoke the two under a repertoire of poetic styles that claimed antecedents in Ashbery, Russian Futurism and *Tender Buttons*. If it is hard not to see a discrepancy between the aims and the achievements of Language poetry, that must partly be because the ambitions were so heroically gargantuan. (And, some might argue, because of a thinness in their poetic models.) If it therefore becomes necessary, as well as easy, to pick holes in Language arguments, it is still worth noting and saluting the enormity of what these poets have wished to write their way into. Their work and the questions it raises form a standing rebuke to the prevailing mediocrity of America's cultural output during the Reagan and Bush administrations.

II

From the outset, one strategy of $L=A=N=G=U=A=G=E$ writing lay in the recognition of the intractability of the tasks in hand, followed by a doubling of the linguistic stakes. If it proved difficult to develop a prose which would operate satisfactorily as a combined theory of poetry, economics and revolution, then that difficulty would be surmounted by a bravura leap, as in this display of acrobatics by Steve McCaffery:

> Grammar is a huge conciliatory machine assimilating elements into a ready structure. This grammatical structure can be likened to profit in capitalism, which is reinvested to absorb more human labour for further profit. Classical narrative structure is a profit structure.

> Grammar, as repressive mechanism, regulates the free circulation of meaning (the repression of polysemeity into monosemeity and guided towards a sense of meaning as accumulated, as surplus value of signification).

To have registered, say, certain parallels between the rise of the bourgeois novel and the expansion of the Industrial Revolution would not have told the reader anything new. The novelty of McCaffery's analysis lies in its internalization of political struggle within a macrocosmic linguistic model. The fight for and against certain kinds of language becomes immediately a struggle for new political arrangements, affinities with roughly contemporary developments such as Deleuze and Guattari's *Anti-Oedipus*, work by Julia Kristeva, and other radical and interdisciplinary approaches being clearly present. As a set of suggestive parallels, the new Language model is at least as plausible as the Europeans' polemic. His failure to convince is tied to McCaffery's unwillingness to concede the element of rhetoricity in his project. He *dare* not, because the scale of Language's ambitions leaves him no option but a double-or-quit gamble on the impressiveness of his own schema. The alleged parallels between economic and linguistic structures become ingenious, overly intricate, and in the end ludicrous.

> A grammatical critique can be mobilized by presenting language as opaque and resistent (*sic*) to reinvestment. A language centered

writing, for instance, and zero-semantic sound poetry, diminishes the profit rate and lowers investment drives just as a productive need is increased.[20]

As Rod Mengham has observed of such 'bursts of legislation' by McCaffery and Bruce Andrews, 'it does not follow that any and every formulation of political economy can be applied in the field of language', even if the general feasibility of a comparison between the workings of language and capital be conceded.[21] Where Mengham detects an excess of confidence in the scope of the comparison, one might just as easily diagnose an equally neo-Shelleyan anxiety. Just so, the breathless conclusion of *Epipsychidion* with its insistence that everything in the linguistic and sexual spheres must and shall intersect leads precisely to their pyrotechnic expiry. There is a long tradition in modern English and American poetry of barely acknowledged, would-be legislation.

The more customary Language position, again contemporary with the arguments of literary theory, is that the various kinds of linguistic dishevelment and terroristic circuit breaking available to poetry belong to, as well as pointing up, social/linguistic reality as a site of incessant contestation and contradiction. This does not prevent the resurgence of fabulously Romantic ambitions such as McCaffery's, which might ultimately be read as over-compensations for the marginalization of poetry within the social arena it so desperately yearns to reconstruct. The early *L=A=N=G=U=A=G=E* manifestos dared not afford to be sceptical. Any such qualities were exiled to the poly- or 'zero-semantic' propensities of the poetry.

Notwithstanding the collectivism of their aims, the practice of individual poets gathered under the Language umbrella shows great variation. Ron Silliman's ongoing multi-volume sequence *The Alphabet* and the minimalism of Craig Watson's work could hardly be further apart in style or procedure. What would seem to unite all these poets, however, is the nature of their interest in the politics of poetic form. This is not confined to questions of purely literary innovation and influence. Language poetry is predicated on the belief that the visible and audible divergence of poetic language from customary discourse does itself mark out the ground of subversive political activity. In one of many calls to the linguistic barricades, Bruce Andrews voices an impatience with the ideological closure implied by single meaning: 'stop repressing the active construction, the *making* of meaning, the *making* of sense – social sense.'[22] The insistence here is not merely on the opening up of the means by which meaning is made; the poem in such a case would resemble one of those high-tech buildings that wears its piping and elevators on the outside – startling, but in no sense out of synch with the capitalist projects it houses.

Rather, as I have shown, the intention of Language is to disclose the workings of linguistic expression so as to open up wider issues of social meaning, by analogy. It is with analogy, imported in order to shrink the distance between poetry and more acknowledged modes of legislation, that the problems appear. As Charles Bernstein announces, in the afterword to the collection of papers from which this chapter draws its subtitle; 'The poetic authority to challenge dominant societal values, including conventional manners of communication, is a *model* (my emphasis) for the individual political participation of each citizen.' Even at its most intensely polemical, Bernstein's writing is characterised by a hyperactive wit recalling the provocations of Dada and Surrealism. His use of modishly ecological imagery to back up the argument about a political relevance for poetry is serio-comic, perhaps, once more, because of an unacknowledged uncertainty about the validity of his argument:

> Poets don't have to be read, any more than trees have to be sat under, to transform poisonous societal emissions into something that can be breathed. As a poet, you affect the public sphere with each reader, with the fact of the poem, and by exercising your prerogative to choose what collective forms you will legitimate. The political power of poetry is not measured in numbers: it instructs us to count differently.[23]

The words used here may bounce off their referential vectors like the energy field in a Kirilian photograph, to adopt an analogy used elsewhere by Bernstein, but the argument gets damaged in the process. Trees don't have to be sat under, arguably, to be trees; but poems, surely, do have to be read. Yet when they are read, the 'fact of the poem' alone seems poor soil from which to expect to see the 'political power of poetry' flourish.

Bernstein has been advancing these same arguments since the late 1970s. 'So writing might be exemplary – an instance broken off from and hence not in the service of this economic and cultural – social – force called capitalism. A chip of uninfected substance; or else, a 'glimpse', a crack ...'[24] A chip, a glimpse, a crack; a 'model' for political participation; there is always, always has to be, a metaphor to bridge the gap between poetry and the world outside it that every socially conscious poet since and including Shelley has strained to bridge. Elsewhere, ironically, the Language poets are only too aware of the unbridgeability of the gap between words and things. Language poets want the political sphere to be an exception to the linguistic rule whose unacknowledged sway their work is otherwise, ironically, so intent on disclosing. To date, the problem for Language has been that of language.

III

Words are always late for the event. Words can point to, describe, sketch, shadow, haunt – do anything but *be* their object. And yet, the act of reference, always doomed to miss its target, still generates linguistic life, which poetry in particular has learned to cultivate; at times, indeed, taking the element of accident or slippage from communicative meaning as its own province. Once again Shelley's poetry is instructive, in part because of his peculiar ability to both enter a delirium of poetic language, but enter in order to critique its limitations. *Epipsychidion* is again a powerful example: it begins by the poet's lancing a hundred verbal epithets at the absent object of thought ('Emilia Viviani'), only to concede their inefficacy:

> I measure
> The world of fancies, seeking one like thee,
> And find – alas! mine own infirmity.

This 'infirmity' becomes, however, the ground of poetic life.

> A Metaphor of Spring and Youth and Morning;
> A Vision like incarnate April, warning,
> With smiles and tears, Frost the Anatomy
> Into his summer grave.[25]

The skewed victories of poetic language, its transformation of the failure of referentiality into the strange triumph of the non-representational, do of course figure prominently in the modern poetry of Europe and America. The precursors claimed by Language writing – John Ashbery, the Surrealists – show this acutely. It would be inappropriate to an introductory study such as this, but perfectly possible to demonstrate a continuing persistence of Romanticism that might include the Language project without either domesticating it unfairly, or collapsing the important divergences of Language from its poetic predecessors.

This chapter will conclude with an enquiry into particular examples of Language poetry, to see if the slippage of signifier from signified, and of poetic language from social reality – which problematises the prose manifestos – can be turned to a victory in poetry, however Pyrrhic or Shelleyan.

IV

The opening poem of a sequence or collection is a traditional locus for the poem about poetry, or about poetry's catalysis; a transitional writing where theoretical prescription and active practice may meet visibly, but only to bid farewell. The two poetic overtures under discussion are the opening page of Bob Perelman's book-length sequence of prose poems, *a.k.a.* (1984), and the first work in a cycle of a hundred poetic texts, *Raik* by Ray DiPalma (1989).

Here is the opening of Perelman's first page:

> I am often conscious, yet rain is now visibly falling. It almost combines to be one thing, yet here I am again. Though he dreamed he was awake, it was a mistake he would only make at a time like that. There are memories, but I am not that person.[26]

and here is the opening of *Raik*'s poem:

> 20 minutes of indolence
> 44 years of speculation
> emblematic pretext five
> flexes or more to tenor
> the specific molded ilk[27]

Such comparisons are invidious, in one sense; an artificial juxtaposition of two texts with no necessary connection, bent into proximity by the exigencies of an outsider's agenda. Yet, one only ever reads for some purpose or to satisfy some particular need, a reality that Language poetry itself has not been slow to note.

The Perelman poem announces at once that it is to be an examination of consciousness. Right from the Cartesian parameters of the opening words, it is clear that this is going to be an enquiry into the phenomenology of perception and consciousness, mind and its objects. That the instances offered to the reader are not going to be self-evidently or conventionally rational is also made an issue from the outset. The first sentence is not constructed as if its second half were a non sequitur, yet it is – at least in terms of conventional expression. The second sentence is similar in construction. The third reverses this approach; apparently a non sequitur, it actually makes experiential sense; the mistake of thinking yourself awake when you are not could indeed happen only in dreams. The final sentence of the paragraph summarises a key theme for the text as a whole: that while the history of a person's memory appears to him or her to be continuous and ongoing, the self is self-divided. You are not now the person you once were, for good or ill, and not merely in terms of the change from a child to an adult, but by implication, from minute to minute, from perceptual scene to scene. Perelman's last phrase replicates the close of a lyric by Frank O'Hara, 'How to Get There':

> and we drift into the clear sky enthralled by our disappointment
>   never to be alone again
>   never to be loved
>   sailing through space: didn't I have you once for my self?
>   West Side?
>   for a couple of hours, but I am not that person[28]

Perelman may or may not be quoting O'Hara, consciously or unconsciously. Either way, his poem establishes itself as in the O'Hara line: that is to say, consciousness-centred in a speculative and exploratory way that will use devices of estrangement, defamiliarization, parataxis and the whole grab-bag of modernist method to both detain the reader's attention, and define the text as poetic.

By contrast, DiPalma's text takes textuality as its dominant subject, *ab initio*. I did not have to forcibly justify the lines as I typed them out just now on my word processor. Each line is exactly the same length, in characters and spaces. There are five lines, and they include the word 'five'. As the first in a sequence of a hundred related poems, this first is in a sense the pre-text, a word that is also included. Form and formalism are very clearly on the poet's agenda, and the rest of the poem, if not the book, is going to be the logical development of a 'molded ilk'. The potential for tonal warmth, or even tonal variation, would seem to have been deliberately abjured to clear the way for an atmosphere of rather strict experiment. In fact, the rest of the poems are of varying lengths, but are equally box-like in form, use a considerable amount of repetition, and frequently open up their first line for recombinant possibilities as each page proceeds. The microscopic attention to words and letters that has always characterized the poetry of Tom Raworth, (who published alongside DiPalma in the days before Language), is the stable basis of the work under scrutiny. The strong implication of *Raik* is the inaccessibility of consciousness outside language – it is literally and purely a language poem.

The texts show certain common interests – in repetition and the recombinant potential of language, and in verbal quirkiness, for example. (It is significant that all the devices they share may be found in the work of Gertrude Stein.) Yet the differences of approach are vital, and rooted in the history of poetry as well as each author's personal style. Here is a later poem from *Raik* in its entirety:

>   overandovergoes
>   formandform'sop
>   acity*is*islateri
>   sitlatertheveil
>   edinsideandoutt
>   oextendtherando

minthewaterstri
ppedofitspatina
rawradiantsurmi
seonelistenandt
wotransformlaug
hedandplacidpeg[29]

The chief limitation of this kind of poem lies in its fealty to a pre-existing theory. Ultimately it is as soluble as a crossword puzzle. Multiple meanings do hang around the fourth line; (is it 'sit later the veil,' or 'is it later the veiled inside'?) but this is not the kind of poetic ambiguity likely to lure one back for repeated rereading. The lack of spacing turns the text into an obstacle course, a retardation clearly intended to stimulate meditation on the working processes of reading and writing which are normally submerged in habit. At this level, it is a mildly instructive essay on 'formandform'sop/acity', though I suspect that most readers could have done with a bit more 'rawradiantsurmi/se'. At any rate, the steps by which one moves from picking out individual words to thinking about more general operations of language are quite clear. In keeping with this, Steve McCaffery notes on the back of the cover of *Raik* that the poems seek to 'resensitize the materiality of words'. His next statement seems more questionable: 'These poems yield primary encounters with orthography and lexicon that induce political beyond aesthetic implications.' Here again is the excessive confidence in poetry's capacities, and its corollary anxiety that any poetry whose aims are less than world-changing has collapsed into aestheticism.

It is significant that Perelman retains while DiPalma abjures methods of approach and stylistic features of the new American Poetry, what Michael Davidson termed 'expressivism'. While DiPalma would seem more engaged by Dadaist, Futurist and Concrete methodology, Perelman maintains a purchase on the consciousness-centred lyricism of Robert Duncan's and John Ashbery's generation. I would argue that there is a general tendency in Language poetry for those texts which are more open to the expressivist heritage to work more successfully than the purist approach, typified by *Raik* or the (to my eyes, barren) work of P. Inman. This holds true within the work of individual poets, also. Stephen Rodefer's *Four Lectures* has a dazzling wit, outshining the later and more programmatic *Emergency Measures*; yet when Rodefer's style seems most his own, it also shows a straight continuity from texts like Ed Dorn's *Gunslinger* and the poems of Frank O'Hara. The remainder of this study will be concerned to test Davidson's claim that Language offers a potent critique of expressivism, alongside the possibility that Language writing at its best actually uncovers unexplored resources in American poetry of the postwar period.

3. Songs of the Self

I

If the New American Poets such as Dorn and Wieners and O'Hara published work that was grounded in an expressive individualism, the burden of particular poems often lay in the disclosure of divisions within the self. The unspeakable visions of the individual, to revive Jack Kerouac's motto for poetry, tended to issue in practice as speakable visions of the individual's not-being. The pleasures of reading the New American Poetry are to be discovered through a paradox: while poets in the 50s wrote under the oblique influence of continental existentialism, a philosophy of loneliness brought home by the activity of producing alienated poetry in a time of Cold War and commercialism, the self-splitting in the poetry can signal the aspects of selfhood that link and overlap in relationships and the social world.

Frank O'Hara's poetry, for example, gives voice to the psychodrama of a self caught between the shaping pressure of will, and the self-opening of desire and the propensity to float into identification with the other. These tensions are often exploded in complex sorts of comedy, rather than resolved, as in O'Hara's most famous poem 'In Memory of My Feelings':

> Grace
> to be born and live as variously as possible. The conception
> of the masque barely suggests the sordid identifications.
> I am a Hittite in love with a horse. I don't know what blood's
> in me I feel like an African prince I am a girl walking downstairs
> in a red pleated dress with heels I am a champion taking a fall
> I am a jockey with a sprained ass-hole I am the light mist
> in which a face appears
> and it is another face of blonde I am a baboon eating a banana
> I am a dictator looking at his wife I am a doctor eating a child
> and the child's mother smiling I am a Chinaman climbing a mountain
> I am a child smelling his father's underwear I am an Indian
> sleeping on a scalp
> and my pony is stamping in the birches,
> and I've just caught sight of the *Niña*, the *Pinta* and the *Santa Maria*.
> What land is this, so free?[30]

No-one but Frank O'Hara could have written this, and the passage would be well-known and probably viewed as a crucial episode by any reader who valued his poetry. Yet this passage, stamped 'O'Hara' as definitively as *Howl* or *Gunslinger* is stamped as the apogee of its author's style, is about the fission of discrete identity into a carnivalesque though alarming democracy of selves. And in broad terms, so is Ginsberg's *Howl*, which pits the 'minds of my generation' against 'Moloch'; and so is Dorn's *Gunslinger*, whose narrative 'I' dies part way through Book II, to make way for less ontologically conventional company. The ultimate discoveries of the New American Poetry carry implications at variance with their neo-existentialist and individualistic stance. One strand of implication leads to a more social poetry which that generation was unwilling to pursue. Social meant societal, and although Dorn, O'Hara and Ginsberg all produced notable anti-racist poems (for example), the ethic and objective remained libertarian, and hence individualistic. By contrast the Language poets were able to draw on the social implications of the New Americans' self-multiplication, encouraged by continental 'theory'. New ways of interpreting selfhood as constructed within a web of interactive codes, set society and the creative powers of language into a new relation. As with the postwar influence of existentialism, French literary theory has had important stylistic and procedural consequences in American Poetry.

Of course the New American Poets did not spring fully-formed out of the Donald Allen anthology. Alongside the influences already mentioned of the San Francisco Renaissance, Surrealism and Modernism, the vernacular objectivism of William Carlos Williams is a ubiquitous catalyst; so is Whitman. The passage quoted from O'Hara's 'In Memory of My Feelings' exists in a clear line of descent from Walt Whitman's great lists, and from his happy conflation of two, seemingly contradictory philosophical positions: rampantly Romantic egotism ('I contain multitudes'), and self-dissolution *into* those multitudes:

> Through me many long dumb voices,
> Voices of the interminable generations of prisoners and slaves,
> Voices of the diseas'd and despairing and of thieves and dwarfs,
> Voices of cycles of preparation and accretion,
> And of the threads that connect the stars ...[31]

Notwithstanding the huge stylistic and other changes since Whitman's time, the same attempts to understand experience through apparently divergent rhetorics of selfhood, nationality, race and gender are canvassed at speed by Frank O'Hara. Of course there are tones in O'Hara that are alien to Whitman: in 'In Memory' comedy is more than tinged with horror, a vertigo at the dissolution of fixed identity, and the lines to do with the arrival of settlers in the New World are shadowed by a historical bitterness howled down by Whitman's booming attempt to sing the unity of dis-united states; as D.H.

Lawrence so tartly noticed. The period when 'In Memory of My Feelings' was written, tends to now be celebrated for an allegedly guileless and Romantic cult of expanded awareness. Much of O'Hara's poetic comedy is a reactive registration of the vertigo such an unsettling, desired but feared, can cause. The poem is about 'how to be *open* but not violated, how *not to panic*' as the painter Grace Hartigan observed.[32] She is the 'Grace' at the beginning of the quoted excerpt, though that whole sentence is chiselled on Frank O'Hara's tombstone: *Grace to be born and live as variously as possible.* The double meaning of the joke shows amply enough the double potential of the poem's discoveries about self, which are also a duplicity. Of all 'my many selves' it is 'the serpent in their midst', cunning and venomous survivor, who must be saved, for poetry's sake. Yet the division of the self can lead to Grace, also.

II

Stephen Rodefer published his first collection of poems in 1965, the year before Frank O'Hara's death, and a decade before Language. Like that of Clark Coolidge and even Ron Silliman, his work might therefore be read as related to, but not circumscribed by either of the two 'generations'. *Four Lectures* (1982) is in no sense a transitional work, but one that both continues directions for poetry inaugurated by O'Hara and his peers, from a coign of vantage informed by the new debates around structuralism and the politics of poetic form:

> In Tehran to show pleasure they throw candy and rose water
> on each other in the street, knowing how.
> A dry, brown mushroom from Menlo Park with no price.
> On his deathbed Breughel instructed his wife to burn some of his
>   (paintings
> as they could get her into trouble, lending personality to his oeuvre.
> Paranoia is a carful. Step into her bed.
>   ('Words in Works in Russian')[33]

What structures the writing's poetic intelligibility is the 'knowing how' that the reader brings from his or her own habitation of the codes that make particular societies at particular times comprehensible. Rodefer's comedy is, in a sense, Saussurean. Any activity is meaningless, in itself, and only given sense by context and convention. (e.g., try throwing 'candy and rose water' over someone in a street in Bellaire, Ohio, rather than Tehran and see if they 'show pleasure'.) The poem's bizarre juxtapositions argue that we should stop making sense, and look instead at how sense is made. The 'dry, brown mushroom' picked in the Park has no price, is not for sale. This small instance of common property has escaped from a particular code, that of commerce; but the mycological memento is not in a state of pure being. Carlos Williams' prelapsarian urge to show the reader a thing as if for the first time looks dated, by this agenda; things and persons are always already constructed by linguistic networks. But like the dying Breughel, the perceptive reader can crack the code and picture alternative arrangements, a propensity that has always got imaginative humans 'into trouble'.

Four Lectures is, in Ron Silliman's words, 'part carnival, part war', a designation that would fit his own work also. His *Sunset Debris* (cf. Rodefer's *Plane Debris*) a thirty-two page text from 1986, is made up entirely of questions:

> Could you hear the violin? Did you go back to smoking? Did you quit the work, half-done, then go back to it, completing a bit at a time? Did it ever occur to you that she might not want it, might have it, might not need it? Did it ever propose itself as a question of privacy? Did you like the colour of the curtains? Did you ever wonder what it felt like, burst of semen into the throat? Doesn't kidney failure haunt you? Can't you foretell arthritis, ulcer, loss of hair, loss of teeth? When will it be your turn for the infarction? Did you see the snow? Did you do the job? Didn't you hope to avoid language that passed itself off as a mockup of consciousness? Didn't you suggest a formula just to get the haters of formulae pissed off? Won't you, given the chance, betray everyone? Did you see how the soldiers, bringing the dead back in body-bags, chew gum?[34]

We are used to reading as interactive, as a process that as it were allows us to get a word in edgeways. We get into some relation with the text in reading, likely to be bored or dismayed by the opposing poles of either an utterly dominant reading, a case of *deja-vu*, or annihilation by the writing. Silliman's text courts the second possibility, a terroristic interrogation that shifts tack with each question. It is an extended reminder of textuality, of the fact that our participation in any text is silent and in a sense imaginary, a fiction. Silliman is attempting a democratisation of categories of experience we might have preferred to keep separate, from those of 'privacy' (sex, bodily dysfunction and disease) to those of the *polis* (war and work). Yet the poet is not in any sadistic sense hidden from view while manipulating the reader. The hope 'to avoid language that passed itself off as a mockup of consciousness' appears self-directed, and would also summarise the projects of Language in relation to O'Hara and the earlier generation. (By referring to them, famously, as his 'I do this, I do that' poems, O'Hara openly conceded the element of 'mockup'.) Silliman, like Rodefer and Perelman, uses the defamiliarizing non sequitur as a shock-effect. But so did T.S. Eliot and Gertrude Stein. What is new here is the shift of poetic ground from the self-consistent authority of the poet's voice, his style or 'mockup of consciousness', to the 'knowing how' through which any statement claims validity.

Style is undoubtedly a casualty of these changes, within the twentieth century understanding of style as modes of artifice whose recurrence guarantees authenticity of personal expression. A reader who prizes the individuality of voice in O'Hara or Olson over the nature of the issues poems raise would undoubtedly see the work of Rodefer et al as related to, but thinner than, the New Americans'. Indeed there is a case (which I cannot quite bring myself to make) for arguing the near irrelevance of any 'issues' to a poetry such as O'Hara's or Charles Olson's. For all the emphasis on history or locale, the reversed Jericho of Olson's aim 'to build out of sound the walls of the city' makes of the *polis* a subjective act of utterance.[35] Just as O'Hara's mock-manifesto 'Personism' does more than mock, so there was more to his objection to 'the serious utterance' than a suggestion that Olson lighten up. The apparently comic utterance can surprise with seriousness, a device exploited constantly by O'Hara, as by Lord Byron before him. It is no coincidence that the dramatic individuation of poetic voice was essential to the practice of both writers.

III

In the more impressive work by Rodefer and Silliman, such as the latter's multi-volume, continuously engaging epic *The Alphabet*, style is an achievement not of voice so much as a primarily visual recording of social signs. Less introspective than the New Americans, and entirely without the tragic lyricism of John Wieners or Jack Spicer, they do still rely more on 'a mockup of consciousness' than the manifestos would care to claim. *What*, a book-length chunk of *The Alphabet*, does this throughout, and superbly:

Zen grocer, Eyes ache
after day at CRT.
A teenage girl with a bright smile,
safety pin through her nose. Bike messenger's
wire basket. Wall up around construction site
with several generations of peeling posters.
Stepping outdoors, the cold air makes my eyes water.
Umbrella handle carved like the head of a duck.
Empire devastates the dominant: End the War

in '94. Patterned white stocking
over thick black ankle. Tremendous
formal *out-thereness* of the haiku
translates into greeting card mush.[36]

What is *What* if not language, late for the event as ever, re-creating
past experience as present? Doubtless the account is not entirely
'faithful', and its true present is the field of the unfolding text: but the
repertoire of recording devices comes straight from Williams and the
Beats. 'Wall up around construction site' omits articles of grammar in
a style – would-be-photographic, impatient for immediacy – learned
from Ginsberg. The interest in haiku is also traditionally San
Franciscan. Indeed,

A teenage girl with a bright smile,
safety pin through her nose.

is virtually using that form, its ways of working not dissimilar to
Kerouac's 'A Haiku':

The little worm
    lowers itself from the roof
by a self shat thread.[37]

Both offer a simple image which is then jerked out of the frame of
readerly expectation by a slightly unpleasant detail of physicality, (the
safety pin, 'shat') which is then accepted as real, and integrated into
the image as an achieved miniature, a haiku. Kerouac's vermiform
triplet is itself one 'self shat thread' of text, a celebration of sturdy
independent life which, without labouring the point, one could read as
consonant with Beat individualism. Silliman's punk girl with safety pin
is a poetic image from a more social world. I suspect that white,
western readers of a certain age and older have never quite got used
to the spectacle of adolescent girls choosing to pierce their noses.
However, to other readers/observers, those below a certain age for
example, the fashion is familiar, and so the two-line image would
operate quite smoothly, without any jerk of incongruity. By such
means the whole force of Silliman's poetic points towards 'several
generations of peeling posters', a history of changing signs. Ron
Silliman may be the first and last major structuralist comedian in the
American tradition.

But if certain techniques employed here build on Beat achievements, there is also a criticism of postwar expressivism at work in
Rodefer and Silliman. The more bardic stretches of Allen Ginsberg
have not worn well, and their fall from relevance has been accelerated

by books like *What* and *Four Lectures*. Here is Ginsberg cruising on the full tank of his own Whitmania, crowned King of the May ('Kral Majales') by Prague's youth in the spring of 1965:

And I am the King of May, which is the power of sexual youth,
and I am the King of May, which is industry in eloquence and
                                    action in armour,
and I am the King of May, which is long hair of Adam and the Beard
                                    of my own body
and I am the King of May, which is Kral Majales in the
                                    Czechoslovakian tongue,
and I am the King of May, which is old Human poesy, and 100,000
                                    people chose my name.[38]

Silliman and Ginsberg write at opposing poles of what is simultaneously a politics and a poetic form. If the revolutionary ambitions of the Language manifestos are put aside in favour of actual poetic practice, the politics implied by the work – which need no manifesto, at least with the stronger poets – become challenging and effective. The ludicrous cosmic preening of Ginsberg's jaunt around Prague is not only a culpable evasion of the political at a site of acute political tension, but a failure of language which the practice of more recent poetry can help us to deconstruct accurately.

Ginsberg is stuck in a view of language as symbolic. Sexuality, comic kingship, the 'Czechoslovakian tongue' and 'old Human poesy' all nest inside each other as translucent symbols, stretching from a Romantically ecstatic first-person singular out to the nebulae. It is a late flowering of Whitman's Transcendentalism, which is a kind of Coleridgean Romanticism, brusquely stripped of its hang-ups and handed a megaphone in the theatre constructed from America's revolution. The Language emphasis on allegory rather than symbol, metonymic urban bric-à-brac rather than grand metaphors of the psyche, the secular rather than the mystical; all combine to deflate the vatic ambition of Beat prophecy and self-absorption while opening up new avenues for a poetry of expanded *social* awareness.

IV

The prominent achievements gathered behind the banner of Language do not exclusively demote the person in order to point towards the social. The work of Lyn Hejinian, particularly *My Life*, brings autobiography and the construction of personality to the fore. This text both builds on and departs from the simple promise of its title, conspicuously omitting the dramatic highlights of the conventional life-narration. *My Life* contains no climactic anecdotes of sexual encounter, motherhood or vocational decision, though the consequences of such absent moments, pivotal in the autobiographies of the famous, are everywhere in the text. Marjorie Perloff sees an element of playful satire in this refusal, writing of Hejinian's work that it 'calls attention to the impossibility of charting the evolution of a coherent "self", the psychological motivation for continued action'.[39] Despite such a lack of forward propulsion, the textual first person is not presented as the passive tabula rasa for the social codes prevalent in her lifetime, though we all are that, intermittently, as the text acknowledges with a dry wit: 'Now that I was "old enough to make my own decisions," I dressed like everyone else.' Instead the prevalent method is a collage of what are arguably non sequiturs, broadly comparable to the techniques sketched in Rodefer and Silliman's work. Their instinctive leaning is towards the brilliant image and the snappy one-liner, however, where Hejinian's characteristic tones are restrained and delicate:

> What a situation. The refrigerator makes a sound I can't spell. The finches have come at last to the feeder. The magician had come to entertain the children at the birthday party. It was called mush, and we ate it for breakfast in patterns, like pudding. We were like plump birds along the shore. Green night divining trees, scooped too. What memory is not a "gripping" thought.[40]

For all the quietness of its immersion in reminiscence, *My Life* is as open-ended as *What* or *Four Lectures* in its aversion from the mockup of consciousness, faked and traditional coherence. Instead the reader is invited to participate in the production of meaning, choosing perhaps to stress the syntactical parallelism in the third and fourth sentences of this extract as the ground of sense: or noting that 'The refrigerator makes a sound I can't spell' uses a child's perceptions to make relatively sophisticated points about the divergence between values of sound and semantics, points that the conspicuous poeticism 'Green night divining trees' underscores in a different way. The work's formal exoskeleton combines restraint and openness in a comparable ambiguity. Written at the age of 37, *My Life* contained precisely that number of sections, each of which was 37 lines long. In republishing the book at the age of 45, Hejinian has stayed true to form, and added the numerically appropriate quota of sections and sentences. The new material fits seamlessly into the old, each chosen life-sentence as opaque and yet open to the construction of meaning as any other.

Michael Davidson argues that in the inevitable attempt by the reader to find connectives where the divergent sentences refuse to yield them readily, opacities and silences may be imbued with qualities intrinsic to the experience of women in society. Taking the juxtaposed phrases 'Women, I heard, should speak softly without mumbling. The obvious analogy is with music.', he remarks:

> The idea that girls should speak softly without mumbling or that one should learn to listen is a bit of adult wisdom whose social consequences have only recently been challenged ... When Hejinian asserts that "the analogy is with music," she refers both to the organisation of her sentences and to the way that women's silence is analogous to the "elusive" properties of music.[41]

The 'elusiveness' of a female voice disenfranchised by the discourse of male authority is of course a topic on which the various feminisms have reached diverse conclusions. Hejinians's is not (as far as I can detect) affiliated to any particular set of prescriptions. Published in its first version in 1980, *My Life* does however appear to both side and take issue with the feminist innovations of the time.

By the late 70s, a loosely deconstructive approach acknowledging the French theorist Luce Irigaray, and stressing the unplaceable place of woman's language as the Other, or unconscious of the male, had become part of American debates. Other, less theoretical and more historicized models were in play, including nineteenth century Methodism, and more importantly the spiritual autobiographies of Puritan women. Language writers such as Susan Howe have been able to make productive use of the latter, but a throughgoing if quiet irony in Hejinian's sense of her own relationship to the meta-narratives of history, collective endurance and progress, appear to make any such affiliation problematic for her. There is undoubtedly a sense in which *My Life* is offered as a confessional text, and can therefore be related to developments of the time within feminism; yet the literary devices adopted by Hejinian are as complex and potentially rebarbative as any in the traditional armoury of male Modernism: straightforward communication is deconstructed satirically as well as embroidered poetically in this *Life*. Her writing appears to run along lines at times parallel to Irigaray's *Speculum*, but to be distanced from psychoanalytic approaches, with their stress on introspection, and the assumption of a unified self. Not only does Hejinian reject the cultic imagery of witches, goddesses and other mythic paraphernalia; thematic representation of women's lives is almost absent from her work. This is a feminist writing, in certain respects closer to the work of Denise Riley in England than to most Language poetry, that abjures formulaic summary of women's biological or economic identity or oppression. In Hejinian's 'rejection of closure', to take the title of an essay by her, speaks an individualistic feminism that sees literary work as determining the criteria by which it is to be read.

Though elusive, Hejinian's work may be more productive than poems by Nicole Brossard or Louise Dupré, whose affiliation to the new French feminism of Hélène Cixous seems all too literal and neat. Language-related in its preferred devices, Brossard's work stresses the enactment rather than description of present experience, only to contradict her own project by gearing it so neatly to a fixed agenda preceding the text:

> the entire skin the fictional skin the epidermis
> deep in her eyes lies the very question of everyday living
> the impression that the lower belly is generating signs
> saliva that substance directly secreted by the exposed
>   body
> like a page full of potentialities[42]

This is a poetry that talks about what it isn't ('crazed with desire'). It might usefully be contrasted with the work of Diane Ward, a body of writing more truly 'full of potentialities'; contemporary with the Cixousian imperative towards poetic corporeality, but not dwarfed by its embrace:

> Last night I was the mouth pressed to the shoulder
> blade at the same time I was the hardest edge
> of the bone itself. I was two figures, no three,
> shrinking away toward the distant line labeled
> horizon, known to trade its place with you.
> The three figures were drawn together twice;
> first, as stick figures or in full perspective
>   on white paper by the hand that's free to dream,
>   clearing the way for the second drawing,
> the moment that imagination always knew could
>   include you, me, and the spectrum of pronouns
>   conducting a conversation as background to
>   the ragged line of isolated bodies moving as
>   one, voluntarily bunched together then released.[43]

The 'spectrum of pronouns', rather than a separatist confinement to the pronouns of what American feminism once termed 'herstory', facilitates a dazzling moiré patterning of subject-positions, using the poem as model for a Romantic desire whose aim is still spillage back into the extra-poetic. Ward's poetry celebrates the 'hand that's free to dream'; as with Hejinian, artistic activity is proposed as a model of what Silliman calls in another context 'unalienated work'. The poem 'stands in relation to the rest of society both as utopian possibility and constant reminder of just how bad things are.'[44] This is perhaps overly ingenious, allowing Language poetry's habitual revival of Modernist devices the luxury of a retrospectively self-justifying choice between utopianism and terrorism, as the necessity arises. A more generous and accurate account might propose that, in a hypothetical triangulation of feminism, Language writing and the heritage of the New American poetry, each might learn from the other – if only from their gaps and omissions.

4. Conclusion: Beyond Language

The social orientation of Language poetry and the model of the avant-garde côterie that was exploited by the New American Poets point equally but differently to ideas of community. The evaluation of the Beat writers current in America, exemplified by Ted Morgan's biography of William Burroughs, *Literary Outlaw*, or the reissue of Kerouac's jazz-poetry as a boxed set (complete with explanatory booklet), scavenges for biographical anecdote filtered through nostalgia. The Beats are, by this account, made mythical; the sex and drugs and angst merely Halloween masks for Tom Sawyer and his gang. The emphases are finally on non-revolutionary lawlessness, peer-bonding, and the utopian 'possibilities of a community in a world dominated by authoritarian elders'. In his definitive account of the relationship between poetics and community at mid-century, *The San Francisco Renaissance*, Michael Davidson remains sympathetic to the writing but intent on deconstructing the myth:

> Within the "enabling fictions" of community surrounding the San Francisco Renaissance can be glimpsed the utopian hopes for some kind of *Gemeinschaft* that was rapidly being replaced by suburban anonymity and the new corporate state. Such fictions do not diminish the integrity of the movement but suggest the difficulties that postwar writers had in separating themselves from the society they criticised.[45]

The North Beach 'scene', Jack Spicer's barroom Round Table, Beat adventures 'on the road' did in one sense vanish as they appeared, mirages driven back by the irresistible advance of consumer capitalism. And yet the vital and massive cultural changes in American culture around the late 60s and early 70s drew directly on the Beat blueprint, and remain the cultural lexicon for nonconformist expression.

Language poetry has inherited the urge towards rebellion, but has had to mount its critique from within the golden age of credit and the shopping mall; dissidence has been bought off. Late capitalism is not the only marginalising force: Language at the theoretical level is, as it were, terribly late socialism, the belated intervention in American literary debates of an informed Marxist perspective. But while the worldwide collapse of communism is unlikely to prevent Ron Silliman from continuing with *The Alphabet*, recent events have hardly brought Language interests and innovations into mass culture, in the ways that brought the Beats a real fame and influence. Instead, radical American poetry has been pushed back into the arms of the University; 'the 500 pound gorilla at the party of poets', in Silliman's choice phrase, and one in whose embrace the would-be revolutionary can at best squirm. But if the number of tenured Faculty members hired directly because of their Language enthusiasms 'can be counted on the fingers of one hand after an industrial accident' – Silliman's Union Card has clearly been countersigned by William Burroughs – it is also the case that 'language poetry is *already* integrated into the institutional discourses of the academy'.[46] Jerome McGann, Marjorie Perloff, Michael Davidson and George Hartley have published important books and articles; and the replies to a questionnaire to poets about employment in a recent issue of *Tyuonyi* magazine suggests that the University is where poets are found, even if it isn't the same poets two years running. ('My job as an adjunct faculty member at UCSD helps keep my family solvent, but, of course, there's no job security', was a typical account.)[47]

And yet the anecdotal evidence from Creative Writing programmes in the States suggests that where Language material has been read, students pick up a single style to be deployed at will. This is confirmed by an instructive anecdote from England. Ken Edwards is the editor of *Reality Studios*, now an innovative press, but until recently a magazine:

> By 1983, I had received, among the many eager unsolicited submissions arriving for *Reality Studios*, one from an American poet who enclosed some Surrealist-style poems with a note to the effect that if I didn't like them this person could send me some in a "Language poetry style", or "like Charles Bernstein". This told me two things : one, the language poets (and Bernstein in particular) had definitely arrived; two, the movement had reached its culminating point or point of failure (that is, when people start imitating its effects without understanding its bases) remarkably early. Since resistance to reification is a central driving force for these poets, such a development gives rise to decidedly mixed feelings.[48]

It may be that an accelerated disposability is now a feature of the life of things, and that a jaundiced and unfairly premature codification of intellectual developments is as built into the system as the 'need' to upgrade your computer, hi-fi, etc. However, if 'the movement' has peaked, perhaps the term 'Language poetry', useful as a handle, should be relegated to the past in order to facilitate getting to grips with what is in truth a provocative variety of poems and poetics.

II

Although the intervention of the new poetry has helped prolong the flagging careers of one or two older practitioners, its influence leaves recent books by the stars of *The New American Poetry* untouched. Robert Creeley's latest collection *Windows* (1991) weighs in at over a hundred and fifty pages, all, alas, focused on the same foreboding at mortality. Even weightier is John Ashbery's *Flow Chart* (1991), a single poem of over two hundred pages. This magnificent and magnificently indulgent work is hardly a sign of diminished energies, but it builds on a repertoire that was running smoothly well before Language. Edward Dorn is probably the poet of his generation to have campaigned with most persistence and vituperation against recent developments; his claims might carry more weight if his own recent *Abhorrences* (1990) were less a series of armchair outbursts, an irritable flipping of the cultural zapper. Having won his spurs, the Gunslinger appears to prefer carpet slippers.

The current impact of the new poetry on British writing is interestingly divergent. In a published lecture on 'Language, Poetry, and Language Poetry' Edwin Morgan draws attention to the importance of Stein, and of Russian Formalist concepts like *ostranenie* to the newest American poetry. However he betrays a very British kind of impatience in chastising the poets for proffering work 'which may be almost but never quite solved', as if the poem were a crossword it would be irritating not to be able to complete.[49] More fertile ground has been tended by a number of relatively fugitive and often university-based journals, from the Oxford-based *fragmente* to *Equofinality* in Cambridge; David Marriott's *Archeus*, Paul Green's *Spectacular Diseases* are also an ongoing archive of Language's effects on British poetry and poetics.

Most of all, however, the literary effect of Language will have been to redraw the map of American poetry after 1945; in part, through the work of Rodefer or Silliman, to add to the sum of texts that repay rereading, but also to show the earlier work in a new light. The 50s generation emphasised the performative and individualistically gestural aspects of poetic writing somewhat at the expense of a social analysis, of a kind which the more recent writers have been able to supply. Whether their attempts to, in Olson's phrase 'write the republic', have produced any single text as powerful as *The Maximus Poems* is another matter. At the least, they further the case that the New American Poetry was, *in toto*, the strongest the republic has produced.

Notes

1. Jerome J. McGann, 'Contemporary Poetry, Alternative Routes', *Critical Inquiry*, Vol. 13, no 3, Spring 1987. p. 643.
2. Rod Mengham, untitled review of Andrews, Bernstein, Coolidge, McCaffery and Watten, *Textual Practice*, Vol. 3, no. 1, Spring 1989. p. 121.
3. Donald Allen, ed. *The New American Poetry*. (New York: Grove Press, 1960).
4. A more extended account of these connexions may be found in Michael Davidson, *The San Francisco Renaissance: Poetics and Community at Mid-Century*. (Cambridge: Cambridge U.P., 1989).
5. See Geoff Ward, *Statutes of Liberty: The New York School of Poets*. (St Martin's/Macmillan, 1993).
6. Davidson, *The San Francisco Renaissance*. p. ix.
7. Edward Lucie-Smith, interview with Frank O'Hara, in O'Hara, *Standing Still and Walking in New York*. (Bolinas, Cal.: Grey Fox Press, 1975). p.13.
8. Frank O'Hara, 'Personism: A Manifesto'. Donald Allen, ed. *The Collected Poems of Frank O'Hara*. (New York: Knopf, 1971). p. 498.
9. Allen Ginsberg, 'City Midnight Junk Strains'. *Collected Poems 1947–1980*. (New York: Harper and Row, 1985). p.458.
10. Steve Benson, *As Is*. (Berkeley, California: The Figures, 1978). p. 1, p. 48.
11. Steve Benson, *Blindspots*. (Cambridge, Mass.: Whale Cloth Press, 1981). p. 9, p. 5.
12. See Steve Benson, *Blue Book*. (Great Barrington and New York: The Figures/Roof, 1988). p. 16 ff.
13. Ginsberg, *Collected Poems*. p. 130.
14. Michael Davidson, '"Skewed by Design": From Act to Speech-Act in Language-Writing'. *fragmente* 2, Autumn 1990, pp. 44–5.
15. As given by Lee Bartlett, 'What is "Language Poetry"?'. *Critical Inquiry*, Vol. 12, no. 4, Summer 1986, p. 742.
16. Steve McCaffery, '*Ow's* "*Waif*"'. (Toronto: The Coach House Press, 1975). Unpaginated.
17. Bartlett, '*What is "Language Poetry"?*', p. 742.
18. Gary Lenhart, untitled review, *L=A=N-G=U=A=G=E* 11, January 1980. Unpaginated.
19. Bruce Andrews and Charles Bernstein, 'Repossessing the Word'. In Andrews and Bernstein, eds. *The L=A=N=G=U=A=G=E Book*.

(Carbondale and Edwardsville: Southern Illinois University Press, 1984). p. x.

20. Steve McCaffery, 'From the Notebooks'. Ibid., p. 160–1.

21. Mengham, *Textual Practice*, p. 119.

22. Bruce Andrews, 'Poetry as Explanation, Poetry as Praxis'. Charles Bernstein, ed. *The Politics of Poetic Form: Poetry and Public Policy*. (New York: Roof, 1990) p. 24.

23. Charles Bernstein, 'Comedy and the Politics of Poetic Form'. Ibid., p. 236 ff.

24. Charles Bernstein, 'The Dollar Value of Poetry'. In *The L=A=N=G=U=A=G=E Book*, pp. 138–9.

25. *Shelley: Poetical Works*, Ed. Thomas Hutchinson (corr. G.M. Matthews) (Oxford: Oxford U.P., 1970). pp. 413–4.

26. Bob Perelman, *a.k.a.* (Great Barrington, Mass.: The Figures, 1984). p. 1.

27. Ray DiPalma, *Raik.* (New York: Roof, 1989) p. 1.

28. *The Collected Poems Of Frank O'Hara*, p. 370.

29. DiPalma, *Raik*, p. 38.

30. *The Collected Poems of Frank O'Hara*, p. 256.

31. Walt Whitman, 'Song of Myself'. *The Complete Poems* (ed. F. Murphy) (Harmondsworth, Middx.: Penguin, 1989 rept.) p. 87.

32. As given in Marjorie Perloff, *Frank O'Hara: Poet Among Painters*. (Austin and London: Texas U.P., 1977) p. 141.

33. Stephen Rodefer, *Four Lectures*. (Berkeley, Cal.: The Figures, 1982) p. 22.

34. Ron Silliman, *The Age of Huts*. (New York: Roof, 1986) p. 32.

35. Charles Olson, *The Maximus Poems*. (Berkeley, Cal.: California U.P., 1983.) p. 600.

36. Ron Silliman, *What*. (Great Barrington, Mass.: The Figures, 1988). pp. 51–2.

37. Jack Kerouac, *Heaven & Other Poems*. (San Francisco: Grey Fox Press, 1987) p. 17.

38. Ginsberg, *Collected Poems*. p. 353.

39. Marjorie Perloff, '"The Sweet Aftertaste of Artichokes": the Lobes of Autobiography: Lyn Hejinian's *My Life*'. *fragmente* 2, p.54.

40. Lyn Hejinian, My Life. (Providence, R.I.: Burning Deck, 1980). pp. 34–6.

41. Davidson, *The San Francisco Renaissance*. p. 213.

42. (Fiona Strachan, trans.) Nicole Brossard, *Surfaces of Sense*. (Toronto: Coach House Québec Translations, 1989) p. 31.

43. Diane Ward, 'Nine-Tenths of Our Body', *Never Without One*. (New York: Roof, 1984) p. 46.

44. Ron Silliman, *The New Sentence*, (New York: Roof, 1987) p. 61.

45. Davidson, *The San Francisco Renaissance*, p. 67, pp. xi–xii.

46. Ron Silliman, 'Canons and Institutions: New Hope for the Disappeared'. In *The Politics of Poetic Form*, p. 157, p. 164.
47. Philip Foss and Charles Bernstein, eds. *Patterns/Contexts/Time: A Symposium on Contemporary Poetry.* (Santa Fe, New Mexico: Tyuonyi, 1990). p.10.
48. Ken Edwards, 'Language: The Remake', *fragmente* 2, p. 58.
49. Edwin Morgan, *Language, Poetry, and Language Poetry.* (Liverpool University, Dept. of Classics & Archaeology: The Kenneth Allott Lectures, No. 5, 1990) p. 5.

Guide to Further Reading

1. Critical Introductions and anthologies

One might begin to find a pathway here by distinguishing between those theoretical or critical texts that have been produced by poets from within the Language movement, (however academic their orientation), and those that have been produced by university-based critics with some pedagogical or other investment in Language.

Chief among the first would be Charles Bernstein's collected essays, *Content's Dream* (Los Angeles: Sun and Moon Press, 1986). Of all the Language poets, Bernstein has been from the outset the most tirelessly willing to provide manifestos, position-papers, and summaries of intent. *Artifice of Absorption* (Philadelphia, Penn.; Singing Horse Press/Paper Air, 1987) is perhaps his most compelling work in this area.

Language began with the journal of that name, edited by Bernstein and Bruce Andrews; their *The L=A=N=G=U=A=G=E Book* (Carbondale: Southern Illinois U.P., 1984) offers a generous selection of reprinted materials, and retains the polemical edge that was so striking about the magazine at the time. Of course Language Poetry is not synonymous with *L=A=N=G=U=A=G=E*, the magazine. However, while there could be endless debate about whether David Antin or Jackson MacLow or a dozen other names should or should not be included within the circle, this book-length gathering of work from the magazine does at least allow a crucial phase of recent American poetry to be presented with coherence and clarity. Also of interest, and also published by Southern Illinois University Press, are *Writing/Talks*, edited by Bob Perelman, and Barrett Watten's *Total Syntax* (both 1985). The transcribed debates in the second are particularly helpful in establishing a theoretical matrix through which the poetry might be read, or taught, now.

There are two outstanding anthologies of Language poetry: *Language Poetries*, ed. Doug Messerli (New York; New Directions, 1987), and *In the American Tree*, ed. Ron Silliman (Orono, Maine; The National Poetry Foundation, 1987). The second has the broader overview. Silliman also contributes one of the liveliest talks in an excellent collection of transcribed papers and discussion, *The Politics of Poetic Form: Poetry and Public Policy*, ed. Charles Bernstein, (New York: Roof, 1990). The contributions by Susan Howe and Nicole Brossard are especially pertinent to an assessment of the relations between feminism and Language.

Ron Silliman's book of connected essays *The New Sentence* (New York: Roof, 1987) will be of help not only to readers attempting to understand Language poetry in relation to wider issues of politics and social change (in which Silliman is both ambitious and helpful), but to those attempting to situate the new poetry in relation to postwar American avant-gardes, as this study has done. The critical use of a term such as 'avant-garde' can never be problem-free, and a book this size lacks the space in which to tackle the various theoretical approaches through which the term has been excavated historically and opened to question in recent years. In some respects, Peter Bürger's *Theory of the Avant-Garde* (Manchester U.P./Minnesota U.P., 1984) remains the most authoritative recent analysis of the term, though that authority has itself been put into question by the recent collapse of classical Marxism, including the belief in historical determinism on which a study like Bürger's rests its case. More promising avenues of enquiry are opened by the Slovenian critic Slavoj Zizek; books such as *Looking Awry* (MIT Press, 1991) throw concepts of high and low art, vanguard and mainstream into a productive turmoil. In a series of related books published over the last ten years, Marjorie Perloff has argued for an understanding of the avant-garde which privileges artistic production over political ambitions; see in particular *The Poetics of Indeterminacy; Rimbaud to Cage* (New Jersey: Princeton U.P., 1981). More recently, Michael Davidson's *The San Francisco Renaissance: Poetics and Community at Mid-century* (Cambridge U. P., 1989) and Geoff Ward's *Statutes of Liberty: The New York School of Poets* (St Martin's/ Macmillan, 1993) are complementary accounts, to the extent that the first looks West for an account of Language's antecedents, where the second draws out the East Coast influences.

The first critical book on Language to appear from inside the university was George Hartley's *Textual Politics and the Language Poets* (Indiana U.P., 1989), which has been joined by Linda Reinfeld's *Language Poetry: Writing as Rescue* (LSU Press, 1992), as this book was going to press. The final chapter of Christopher Beach's *ABC of Influence: Ezra Pound and the Remaking of American Poetic Tradition* (California U.P., 1992) is also of relevance, and brings into focus the relationship between Language and Modernist writers such as Pound and Gertrude Stein on which this essay has only been able to touch.

As readily available to readers with access to a university library will be the occasional articles in *Critical Inquiry* on Language poetry and related topics, particularly Lee Bartlett's 'What is "Language Poetry"?' (Vol. 12, no.4, 1986), Jerome McGann's 'Contemporary Poetry, Alternate Routes' (Vol. 13, no. 3, 1987), and a typically provocative and mercurial offering from Charles Bernstein, 'Optimism and Critical Excess (Process)' (Vol. 16, no. 4, 1990).

Several British journals of poetry and criticism have produced special 'Language issues', of which *fragmente* 2, 1990, has been the best so far. (*fragmente* is edited from Trinity College, Oxford, by Anthony Mellors and Andrew Lawson, who continue to show a commendably un-Oxonian intrepidity in the field of contemporary poetry.) A special issue of *Verse* (Vol. 7, no. 1) guest-edited by Jerome McGann, seemed by contrast more interested in domesticating its chosen materials within a Great Tradition.

2. Poetry:

To dilate at length on which of the many names associated with Language poetry are most worth reading would be to repeat the argument of this brief study. At the time of writing however, it would misrepresent the currently lively condition of American poetry not to cite the work of Steve Benson, Ron Silliman, Stephen Rodefer, Bob Perelman, Diane Ward, Lyn Hejinian and Craig Watson, as the basis of a reading programme. There are a number of poets about whom this study has had little or nothing to say for reasons of space, rather than any critical objection, and these would certainly include Mei-Mei Berssenbrugge, David Bromige, and poets with an investment in minimalism or programmatic repetition, Aram Saroyan, Tom Clark and John Giorno, respectively. A full-length history of Language writing would certainly want to take more account of the work of Clark Coolidge and Michael Palmer, two 'elders' of the movement, than I have been able to do here.

Nationality was another consideration. Language has become a more purely American phenomenon than was true in the relatively fluid context of the late 1970s and early 80s. The work of a major Canadian poet, Christopher Dewdney, and (to my eyes) Britain's greatest poet, Tom Raworth, run as it were on parallel tracks to Language, and might frequently be thought to overtake it.

Both poets are published, like so many Language poets, by Geoffrey Young's press The Figures (5 Castle Hill, Great Barrington, MA 01230). One angle of entry to this material might legitimately be through its presses – The Figures, Roof or Something Else – as much as authors' names. The Figures has led the way since the 1970s, in standards of imaginative book production as well as editorial policy.

Another door which a more substantial history might have opened, but which it must be left to the reader to unlock, would have let in the visual and auditory contributions of Concrete and Sound poetry, respectively. Both intersected with Language, to some degree; just as the New American Poets of the 1960s were influenced by the implications of multi-media experimentation by John Cage and others, so the present-day inheritors of that poetry have been alert to the changing technology of recorded sound, and other developments coming from outside literature. 'Language' is one segment in a kaleidoscope of American experimentalism.

3. Access to Sources:

Although Language material is beginning to find its way on to the British syllabus, access to primary materials can be difficult, outside London. Paul Green, *Spectacular Diseases*, 83B London Road, Peterborough, Cambs., is the official UK distributor of most of the books mentioned in this study, and an excellent source. The following booksellers are among those who stock Language material on a regular basis, and who will deal by post: Compendium Books, 234 Camden High Street, London NW1 6QS; Alan Halsey, The Poetry Bookshop, 22 Broad Street, Hay-On-Wye, via Hereford, HR3 5DB; Peter Riley, 27 Sturton Street, Cambridge CB1 2QG. Waterstone's are getting there.

BAAS PAMPHLETS IN AMERICAN STUDIES

1. SLAVERY
by Peter J. Parish
Recent literature on the subject of black American slavery and the
present understanding of 'the peculiar institution'.
ISBN 0 9504601 2 5   48 pages

2. PROGRESSIVISM
by J.A. Thompson
The various forces behind progressivism and why it was less
successful in the first 15 years of the 20th century than has been
assumed.
ISBN 0 9504601 1 7   48 pages

**3. THE PRESIDENT AND THE SUPREME COURT:
NEW DEAL TO WATERGATE**
by John D. Lees
Analysing the relationship between the American Presidency and
the Supreme Court from 1933 to 1974.
ISBN 0 9504601 3 3   48 pages

**4. THE METROPOLITAN MOSAIC: PROBLEMS OF THE
CONTEMPORARY CITY**
by Philip Davies
The options open to city policy-makers aiming to solve the social
problems that co-exist with wealth and excellence.
ISBN 0 9504601 4 1   48 pages

**5. A SADLY CONTRACTED HERO: THE COMIC SELF IN
POST-WAR AMERICAN FICTION**
by Stan Smith
Post-war American fiction's new model hero and his comic
ambivalences as demonstrated in a selection of novels.
ISBN 0 9504601 5 X   40 pages

6. THE AMERICAN DREAM
by Robert H. Fossum and John K. Roth
Reflecting on the writings of representative American figures to ask
what is the American Dream now that even its recurrent themes
have been called into question.
ISBN 0 9504601 6 3   44 pages

7. THE WELFARE STATE IN AMERICA 1930–1980
by James T. Patterson
The development of the American Welfare State and the evolution
of its policies aimed at reducing poverty.
ISBN 0 9504601 7 6   44 pages

22. VIETNAM: AMERICAN INVOLVEMENT AT HOME AND ABROAD

by John Dumbrell

From the perspective of the post-Cold War 1990s, this pamphlet offers a new synthesis and examination of how America became involved in Vietnam, why she lost the war, and how it should be interpreted.

ISBN 0 946488 12 6   48 pages

23. HARD-BOILED DETECTIVE FICTION

by Ralph Willett

Tracing the evolution of the genre to today's flexibility (which permits different ideological positions), and observing its ability to express themes central to modern American literature.

ISBN 0 946488 13 4   64 pages

24. RADICAL THEATRE IN THE SIXTIES AND SEVENTIES

by Richard Walsh

An examination of the achievements and failures of the radical theatre, comprehending them in terms of the strategies by which it consistently sought to subvert or transcend the prevailing dualisms of its aesthetic and political concerns.

ISBN 0 946488 14 2   48 pages

25. LANGUAGE POETRY AND THE AMERICAN AVANT-GARDE

by Geoff Ward

A lively and comprehensive introduction to the work of such poets as Steve Benson, Ron Silliman and Charles Bernstein, showing the extent to which the 'Language' poets have re-drawn the map of modern American poetry.

ISBN 0 946488 15 0   48 pages.

26. IN NATURE'S DEFENCE: CONSERVATION AND AMERICANS

by Peter Coates

This pamphlet traces the emergence of conservationist thinking, its evolution into the conservation movement, and its progress until the birth of environmentalism. It reveals the diversity of meaning and the historical process of internal conflict and changing identity.

ISBN 0 946488 16 9   56 pages

FOR ORDERING DETAILS PLEASE SEE OVERLEAF.

The current (1993) cost of individual pamphlets is £3.95 except Nos. 23 and 26 which are £4.95.

RYBURN BAAS AMERICAN LIBRARY

The classic of plantation slavery rediscovered —

DRED:
A TALE OF THE GREAT DISMAL SWAMP
by Harriet Beecher Stowe
Edited by Judie Newman

752 pages, 174 x 115mm
Paperback ISBN 1 85331 038 7
Bonded Leather ISBN 1 85331 025 5

The Ryburn BAAS American Library is a reprint series of significant but difficult-to-obtain texts freshly edited by experts specially selected by Ryburn Publishing in association with the British Association for American Studies

ORDER BAAS PAMPHLETS AND RYBURN-BAAS BOOKS
FROM YOUR BOOKSELLER OR DIRECT FROM

RYBURN DISTRIBUTION,
Keele University, Staffordshire ST5 5BG, England

Payment by Access/MasterCard and Visa is accepted: please quote credit card number, expiry date and address at which registered. Credit cards will be debited in £ sterling prices on dispatch of order. If not paying by credit card, non-account customers must enclose payment with order. Postage and packing is charged extra at 10% retail value of order with a minimum charge of £1 and a maximum of £2. Pamphlet orders may be combined with orders for Ryburn books.